THE PRIDE OF LIONS

THE PRIDE OF LIONS

Joon

ERIC
BLOO
DAXE

BLOODAXE BOOKS

Copyright © Joolz 1994

ISBN: 1 85224 294 9

First published 1994 by
Bloodaxe Books Ltd,
P.O. Box 1SN,
Newcastle upon Tyne NE99 1SN.

Bloodaxe Books Ltd acknowledges
the financial assistance of Northern Arts.

For Justin, Warren and The Family.
My thanks, as ever, to the Goddess.

Cover printing by J. Thomson Colour Printers Ltd, Glasgow.

Printed in Great Britain by
Bell & Bain Limited, Glasgow, Scotland.

Contents

7   The Pride of Lions
9   No Memorial
10   Minuet
12   Black Dog
15   Shapeshifter
16   Blam Blam Blam
18   The Perfect Couple
20   Just a Life
22   Root and Branch
24   You're My Friend
25   Going Back
26   Not Waving
28   The Lilac
30   Starlings
32   Fuel to the Flame
34   Nightdrive
36   The Ballad of Steve and Joe
38   Out
39   Memory of family
40   Romeo and Juliet
42   Bradford Again
44   The Boy Nextdoor But One
46   Forgiveness
48   No Place Like Home
50   The Affair
52   Kings of the World
54   Tracy
56   I Did It My Way
58   The Velvet Glove
60   Ghost
61   Falling
62   May
64   Last Words...

The Pride of Lions

Like a great black bubble bursting, he swelled back into consciousness, feeling first the tightened scarlet agony of pulling a breath against broken ribs.

He felt the dusty slick of tarmac under his cheek and he swung dizzily between waking and fainting, unable to understand where he was, or why he was laid on the floor...he could hear Trina shrieking, the high searing screech buzzsawing into his blossoming pain; *shut up shut up, you silly cow,* he thought; *Trina, for God's sake, what's happened?* He tried to speak, but only heard a groaning mumble he realised vaguely was himself; he tried to sit up but could only shudder. He felt a hand on him and a low male voice say:

'You'll be all right, lad, ambulance is on its way, just stay still now, there's a good lad...fucking hell, they've messed 'im up good an' proper the little sods...'

His eyes, sealed shut with bruises, let him roll back in on himself: *they hit me from behind, those bastards from the bar, they got me as we left, I don't believe it, for a spilled drink, Jesus, they can't have been over 16 any of 'em, I don't believe it...*he recalled the narrow white face and stony grey eyes of the youth whose beer he'd jolted; laughing, he'd offered a replacement, secure in his strength and careless. He was 28, fit, he never thought twice about a skinny kid still spotty with adolescence, but the boy hissed at him, his face contorted and full of uncontrolled hatred, the obscenities reflexive and vicious, the weasel pack of his mates chittering with drugs and booze...Trina had clutched his arm, her long false nails biting through his cotton shirt:

'Gary, Garr-ee...let's go, please, let's be off, I don't like it, come *on...*'

And he'd shrugged, turning away from the boy's abuse. Trina teetered out and he followed, anything to please her, his attention focused solely on the jiggling globes of her arse under the tight white dress she'd bought on their holiday in Cyprus, the bounce of her pompom of bleached perm; desire made him stupid and he never noticed the boys come after him, out into the pub car park.

Later, after the hospital and the hopeless mutterings of the police, when he realised nothing was going to be done for him, he spent hours planning elaborate revenges, he and his friends sitting over warm lagers having machine-gun conversations about how these young 'uns had no fear, no respect, they cared about nothing and no one but themselves; they talked and talked, but uneasily, no one did anything. Gary fretted and twisted in frustration yet it seemed tomorrow, always tomorrow would be the day of his great vengeance. He was puzzled and savage with unhappiness, punching his scarred hands into fists; he went on while Trina sighed, fixed her lipstick and trotted out with her friends. When she began not to come back of a night he hardly noticed, his mind rolling on a single track...he knew who they were, at least, he knew their elder brothers, men he'd been to school with, he knew their drinking haunts, their addressses on the maze-like estates where they lived; he went over and over what he would do, obsessed, oblivious, until one day, after work, Trina finished with him.

'Gary love, I just can't stick it any more, it's not right the way you're going on, you should just let it go, drop it, it's drivin' me crackers, honest. Look, I 'ope we can be friends but, well, it's just ovver, that's all...you're just not the same lad any more, you're really not...'

The door shut on the receding clatter of her high heels and he looked at himself in the hall mirror, his broad face with its crooked nose a stranger's face, unshaven, shadowed... not the same lad any more, not the same...and slow tears, hot and shameful to him, trickled down his cheeks while he began to admit no justice would be his, because out in the streets of his own town, new young lions roared and he had nothing to do but lick his wounds, defeated, as age and fear took his body and his heart. Broken, as most men come to be, he finally understood not he, nor anything else in his life, would ever be quite the same again.

No Memorial

She washed the dead child with her own hands, unwilling in the flat shadowless light of the hospital to give the boy up to strangers; turning the cooling limbs as she cleaned them, their sturdy innocence slowly petrifying, the moonstone beads of soapy water tracing the dear familiar curves of arm and breast.

She had brought his new clothes, their jaunty colours jangling against the institutional white sheets, and she dressed him in his best so no one could say he was neglected in any way, not in any way. Her smoothing and tending were fierce with the passion of finality and farewell, and it seemed that nothing else mattered at that time, except the way his soft gold hair made a cowlick on his forehead and his translucent lashes spiked with damp against his rounded cheek. His name she chanted like a charm against his going, over and over under her breath as she worked, the adult sibilance of its cadence a prayer to a black depth she both loathed and needed; no human comfort relevant or useful in this cauldron of pain.

'It's not so much he's gone,' she said to the nurses as they brought her the tea she couldn't swallow, 'I wouldn't mind him being somewhere else, Australia or something, as long as he was in the world somewhere, do you understand, as long as I knew he was breathing somewhere, even if I couldn't never see him again. But this, it isn't fair, he's only little, how will he manage...'

They gave her drugs for her suffering, but she refused them, and muttering his name, fell into the sleep that was the echo of her boy's long journey.

Minuet

She smiles the smile of someone being a bit naughty, downcast eyes, the lashes blobbed with navy blue mascara. Her lips curve like a secret and she flushes a little, bloodrush pink and twists the gold creole in her ear. You would think she'd overspent in the lingerie department, eaten a chocolate too many or flirted with the boss, but it's none of these, nothing that uncomplicated.

It's Kieran: he's due out on bail today and she's got two big lads, friends of her brother's, up at the house for when he gets drunk in town and then comes round to beat the living shit out of her, as he put it on the phone. He's got a real temper, bang, off like a gun he is, no stopping him, not that you'd know if you weren't going with him. An angel in the street, a devil in the house, as they say. His Mam thinks the world of him, never believes a word against him, but then, he always was a smooth talker; fooled her until he moved in and she saw the other side of his nature. It was like walking on eggshells every night, all it took was a wrong look and off he went; she can't remember how many times the police were round; terrible.

Anyhow, he's doing his nut because she wouldn't give him a reference for the court, you see; she didn't fancy him back for Christmas after he was nicked for thieving that Range Rover, stupid sod, not the first time and probably not the last, knowing him. Of course, you know, there was that nice bloke she'd met at the pub, as well... Kieran is such a liability, it'll be windows through, neighbours out, the coppers, everyone screaming, shouting, the baby howling...come to think of it, perhaps the kiddy ought to go to her Mam's. Kieran has a real thing about that child, it would piss him off no end if little Jade wasn't there. Not that she's his, but she's always been his princess, his darling, enough to make you sick, honestly. Her real dadda legged it two months after the birth, that's why she fell in with Kieran, she was at an all-time low and there he was, the original brown-eyed handsome man. Hah! What a mistake...

It's like some strange, formal dance: advance, retreat, turn, bow to your partner. Our mouths say things, the things expected of us but our eyes tell the unacceptable truth. I say, how awful, how horrible, and she says, yes, it's dreadful, in't it and we both know how much she's looking forward to the fight, how she's gearing herself up like a boxer for the contest, a real bit of excitement. All that adrenalin making the heart beat and the brain whirl, a chance to get it all out, all the dross from a life of small tediums burnt away in a flash of passion as vivid as a flame; crying, panting, repeating the tale for weeks and the black eye to prove it; the child's unhappy face and shaky little hands an unnoticed price, a casualty of war.

I've never been out with a bloke that didn't hit me, have you? she says.

No, I say, I haven't.

She lights a cigarette, content in herself. They're all the bloody same, she says.

Yes, I say.

We stare out of the window, it's raining.

And we're all the bloody same, too.

Black Dog

Sometimes I cry so much I can't breathe,
snot bunging up my nose and my chest heaving,
lungs too expanded.
But even when I cry like that I am aware,
I know what I look like... not vanity...
I remember my mother saying
how awful I looked when I cried,
or at least I think I remember, perhaps
I just think I remember, a lot
of my memory is like that; there are gaps,
and then the memories I have seem
like stories belonging to someone else.
I never see through my eyes in memory
but from outside I see myself.

Things hurt me so much.
Other people's lives portrayed on film –
I'm nearly crying now,
I've cried on and off all day, it's the solitude.
I find it too hard to explain how much
I hate being alone. It terrifies me,
each day a regiment of time to get through
all woven about with fear and demons... always fear.
I always have the telly on because of voices,
at least then there are human voices to listen to,
otherwise the demons come and frighten me,
I jump at every sound, a log cracking in the fire,
a car driving down the street...
I am ashamed to say how scared I get,
cowardice, the greatest sin possible,
squats croaking and pointing at the crawling worm
spineless and abased... I *will* not be a coward,
but I am. I always have been.
It's fear that makes me too aware of
other people's rage and pain.
At this very second someone is murdering
someone else, mutilating them, hurting them
in ways it's all too easy for me to feel.

Someone else is dying, racked
and vomiting with cancer, and those
who love them are eaten up with grief,
a child is screaming for a nightlight,
an old woman weeps alone and cold in her room,
the husband she made a pact with all
those long years ago, dead and buried,
and all her children are scattered and uncaring.
She waits for Death to take her hand.
I feel them all, pressing against the walls,
their jabbering voices and their formless pain.

Some days the world recedes and I walk through town
as if someone had turned the sound off on the film;
mouths work, eyes stare but it is very far away.
I speak to shop assistants carefully because I really
want to get it right... seem normal, pleasant, brave.
As always, I watch from outside, I see myself
walk down hills in a black dress, too large and peculiar.

That's when they visit me, the dead, my dead.
Dan's face, chalky and thin, he asks me
to come with him, but he hangs in the darkness
like an ink drawing. And is his desire
because he cannot leave the place he's in?
He invites me and often there is
little enough to hold me, but I haven't gone yet,
Death will come anyhow and I'm too lazy
and too afraid to summon Him out of season.
Dan is disappointed in me, he hung himself,
the one and only blond boy,
no note, he's shaking his head, no note.
I have composed my note a million times
since I was 10. It reads:
'Dear Friends, I'm sorry to upset you like this,
but I really can't wait for the Party any more,
please forgive me, it was no fault of yours but it's all too much
and it may as well be sooner than later... goodbye.'
I have it all planned,
the plastic sheet over the mattress,
the wads of sanitary towels for the disgusting
emptying of the body, the incense burning
to disguise the smell, the clothes laid out

(I shall do it in an old frock),
everything tidy, I have no wish to distress,
boys are so squeamish, I don't feel as though
I would be missed. Dan, my Nans,
Auntie Mitzi, Steve, beckoning, beckoning.
They're not cruel, it's just for company
and I don't blot them out like most,
especially not at night.
I was always scared of the dark.

Death is bold and savage but a gentleman,
perhaps the ideal lover, sardonic, lean and clever,
all velvet, wicked and amusing he will pursue
only me, despite having his choice of lovers,
it will be me he prizes. He will not notice
my faults but find them virtues, boredom will not
flicker behind his wine dark eyes, my tears will be
his crystals and his hand will draw me gently
from the earth, happy at last, freed of guilt
and responsibility, those iron chains that bite
into me daily and poison my blood, that shout
the old refrain, *Not good enough, not good enough!*
Don't work hard enough, don't look pretty enough,
don't do the housework properly, don't grow up,
you are obnoxious, bullying, fat and loud,
always wrong and stupid, always tactless, always whining,
always overbearing, uncaring of other people's wishes,
Selfish, you are a selfish little girl, and
Greedy, a greedy pig, what are you?
A greedy pig, Mummy, a selfish greedy pig
always thinking of myself and making
your life Hell. Did you ever like me, Mother?
I know Father does, sometimes,
if I don't make a fuss and talk about books...
And yes, I know the Golden Rule, Mummy,
People aren't interested in your silly problems.
I know, I see it in their well-meaning eyes,
but,

I am tired of myself... I am tired but I cannot sleep.
I am tired of myself... and get no rest.

Shapeshifter

You know when you dream you've woken up and believing you're awake, your dream is more real than reality...well, it happened to me last night and I dreamt I woke with a start; sweating and staring into the squares of moonlight that bisected the floor, I saw it waiting again. The silver air glittered across its great, unblinking eyes, the slit pupils blooming into black ovals, shadows of the abyss, unreadable. It was, in the dream, much, much larger than in life, it sat on its haunches, pallid; gleaming fur banded and spotted milky white, its huge cat head swivelling towards me with a machine's precision, the tufted ears twitching. Under its animal mask, something else watched; I could see the yellowed ivory beneath the shivering lip, smell the rank meat on its breath, feral, awful, a shining thread of spit spidering to the quilt as it gathered itself to... I screamed and screamed, savage with terror, the noise splitting the world like an axe blow; but it was all a dream; as I really woke, jerking and gasping, you lay still and pure like a marble angel, the rhythm of your breathing untroubled.

While I watched you sleeping, I thought, it was you it wanted, not me; you were the one who ran after it when we saw it on the moor that night, a great, pale cat, obviously an escapee, a bobcat or a lynx living off lambs and rabbits in the heather scrub and the cold, keening wind. There have been lots of sightings of such things, and there it was, ghost-like, unnatural in the thick dark. I said, leave it, leave it, I don't like it, but you followed it like an entranced child as it sat, oddly, waiting, at the top of the hill... and in the steadiness of its intent there was a coldness not truly animal, so fear gripped the back of my neck and I made you come back, while the creature watched...

Now, you can believe or not as you choose, but I tell you this: there are things we don't know of in places we wouldn't suspect, all that is familiar to you may one day warp in the passing of a second into strangeness and chaos; and knowing all, we understand nothing...

In the dream, in its returning, it was you it wanted, not me. Your innocence and consenting, not my knowledge and refusal.

Blam Blam Blam

Two boys cut in front of her in the queue; precisely dressed in the right new "old" clothes, they walk carefully, so as not to shatter their cool. They don't notice her, she's not cool, she's a lame dog; so they cut in front of her, not seeing her, looking, but not seeing.

She's not surprised, doesn't react, it's what she's used to, being invisible, it's natural; her Mam didn't notice her when she was a babby, either; so much so, the social services took her away and gave her to a foster home before she starved to death. Her Mam was pretty feckless, seemingly.

'Runs in the family I expect,' her last Fostermam always said, 'Look at the state of you, wake up for God's sake, Janice, before you get yourself run down crossing the road.'

She liked her last Fostermam though, she liked the house and even the baby retard they brought in after her, but she had to go eventually, couldn't live there forever.

'You'll come back and see us, won't you Jan love, won't you? We'll miss you...'

But she never did; well, hadn't yet anyhow. Meant to, but hadn't got round to it. The days just seemed to run together into one big blob of dole office, social, TV and the romance novels she liked. Which was why she was here, at the big library, having lost *Sea of Passion* a while back and now having a snotty letter about paying for it or something, which she didn't understand. So she was in the queue, and the boys pushing in front of her.

She waits, shifting from foot to foot while the boys try to get tickets and fail, not having I.D. with them and they get ratty with the desk lady. Jan never gets ratty with officials because her whole life of eighteen years has been in their care. She doesn't get ratty with anyone because she doesn't get that worked up over anything; not even when Fosterdad Number Three took her drawers down and shoved his fingers in her, she just sicked up over him, sort of a reflex, she expects. He didn't bother again and she didn't think to tell anyone: par for the course, as Fosterdad Four always said about everything. So is being queue-jumped and having buses drive past you in the pissing rain.

Eventually, snarling puppydog snarls and lathering the air with expletives, the boys steam off, and Janice steps up, the desk lady ignoring her as she tidies her pens in a flustered way and adjusts her big specs over her flushed face. Jan waits. After a minute, the desk lady says *oh!* in a surprised way, and, *yes, may I help you?...* Janice ignores this, knowing that the desk lady means nothing at all by that phrase, and begins a long, complicated story about *Sea of Passion*, but as expected, the desk lady interrupts and says 'I'm sorry' in a voice stuffed with irritation: 'I'll have to fetch Mrs Crossley, lost books are her department, if you'll just wait a moment, please.'

Jan sits back in the squeaky chair and slides her thumb into her mouth, a habit that has bucked her teeth and whittled her thumb into a fleshy lollypop; her hazel eyes half close behind the speckled greasy lenses of her glasses and she drifts into the limbo of half sleep that always overcomes her when waiting for officials. Eventually, she tells her story three more times, never getting to the bit about leaving the book in a Morrisons carrier bag on the 613, while various ladies in blouses struggle with her about paying for the book. Janice gives them some of the money and they hold her card for ransom; all the blouseladies find her unnerving in a way they can't explain and are glad to see the back of her. Jan doesn't notice, and certainly wouldn't care if she did; all officials are like that, it's the way it is. She's a bit sick about the cash, though, it's not like they'd miss one book out of so many, but officials always kick up a fuss about little things and ignore the big things, in her experience.

Outside, the boys are vandalising a bicycle under the tortoise gaze of OAPs who prop themselves on the benches outside the library; they don't notice Jan, any of them. Sometimes she stares at herself in shop windows, mildly surprised to see a reflection. She wishes vaguely she had a big gun like the bloke on telly last night who shot all those people in America, then she'd shoot the boys and the blouseladies and the OAPs and the nasty Fosterdad and her landlord and the dolepeople and the bus drivers who slash past her in the wet and the stupid barking dogs next door and the flasher in the flats opposite and everyone really, except her last fostermam and the poor little baby retard. Yes, she'd shoot all of them, *blam blam blam.* She snorts to herself with laughter and it startles the boys who snap, 'what you laughing at, slag?'

She walks away. Oh yes, *blam blam blam...* all of them.

The Perfect Couple

Linda sits on the ugly stone bench, the icy breeze threading itself through her old combat jacket, while she watches Jamie pretend to play the guitar as he squats on the pavement outside C & A. He isn't even trying to play a tune, just hitting the strings at random and doing what Linda calls his 'superior sod' expression. Not that she'd say that to his face of course, it wouldn't be worth the trouble – he takes himself very seriously. Every now and then, someone who isn't paying attention throws a coin into Jamie's old baseball cap and he glances at Linda with his eyebrows raised as if to say: 'You see, they're such stupid wankers, I'll get money easy, it's a piece of piss...'

Which is what he said last night when Nick and Tony were round and they'd smoked a bit of hash and drunk the bottle of wine Sally had given her ages ago. She'd been saving it for a special occasion ...a special occasion... Linda rubs her cold little hands together and bites a nail down even further, while she wonders just what a 'special occasion' might be. The birthday last Saturday had been her 21st: she'd thought that was a bit special, but Jamie had forgotten, or said he had with that clever clever, don't start look... of course Linda knew perfectly well that he just couldn't be bothered to get her a present and, in a weird way, it was his means of demonstrating to her his much talked about independence. Everyone had asked her what he'd got her, so she made excuses for him like usual, and said he was saving for something really nice, you know, money being tight and all that. It was all rubbish and she was sure everyone knew the truth and was feeling sorry for her, so she'd gone stupidly red and gabbled on too much...she'd felt such a fool. He'd had some money that week as well, but as she lay in bed last night listening to the hard loud laughter echoing up from the living room as the lads got out of it, she knew where it had gone...

'God!' he'd said, when she cried, 'you want to tie me up in this fucking flat don't you? We may as well be fucking married the way you go on...look, if I want me mates round, if I want to go out on me own, if I want to bugger off to Mexico tomorrow I fucking well will, OK? Get it? You're not trapping me in this domestic crap, so shut it and go to sleep can't you, I'm knackered.'

The next day, hung over and feeling a bit guilty, he said: 'Why don't you come with me while I relieve some straight bastards of their loose change, eh?'

She didn't reply immediately, which always annoyed him.

'You don't have to, if you're going to be like that, I'll go on my own... oh, cheer up for Christ's sake, it'll be a laugh...'

She had fixed a nice expression on her face, sticking it on, she thought, like a sticky plaster, something she did a lot these days and being very careful not to irritate him, she followed him into town.

She nodded and smiled as he ranted on, his unshaven face sallow with bitterness and that terrible underlying puzzlement that only Linda ever saw, that child's whine of 'it's not fair' that dogged every thing he did. She could see it in him: why wasn't everything as he wanted it to be? Why didn't he get what he wanted straight away? Why wasn't Linda like the girl he'd had in France that time he went dossing about Europe, who was beautiful, cool and did her own thing? Why, why, why?

Linda twists uncomfortably on the unforgiving stone, watching Jamie in his dirty old clothes, his long bony legs folded up under him, that ugly sneer twisting his mouth, and she sighs and starts to chew the inside of her cheek. She thinks, she could get up now, walk across to him and say: 'Oh, Jamie, by the way, I've decided to have a change, I've decided to fuck off to Mexico, see a bit of the world; in fact, I'm leaving you, you wear me out with your attitude, I'm bored with you so I'm going, ta ta...'

His face! It'd be a total study! She could just see his jaw drop and the disbelief wash over his gritty eyes...but, you know, it was an idea, she could be free, free of him and his idiot friends, free to live for herself for a change, like his ideal girl in fact. But at that moment he stops strumming and tiredly runs his long fingers through his straggly hair in a gesture that she knows so well, his face momentarily soft and unguarded, his expression the same as when they'd first met and he'd wanted her so much. Linda takes two cigs out of her bag and lights them, then gets up and walks over to Jamie.

'Here you are popstar,' she says, and as he takes his, he looks up at her, vulnerable for an instant before the shutters drop over his face again and Linda knows she isn't going anywhere, because she loves him and he isn't as bad as some, he could be worse. No, she isn't going anywhere and despite the big talk, neither is Jamie ...a coin clinks into the hat...

'Tea break,' says Linda. 'Look, all of two quid at least!'

And at last she understands, somewhere inside herself, a secret that Jamie would never know, with his heart breaking, whistling-in-the-dark self delusion, that love isn't pity, but often, for the likes of her, it's very close to it.

Just a Life

We met him in this little leather and goth shop at Camden Market. I'd gone to get some stage clothes made in the goth part, and he was serving in the leather half, which he did when he wasn't sewing. We got on straight away; we used to pop in often after that and he'd come round to our place. His name was Michael, but we never called him that: 'Call me Auntie Mitzi, I'm your auntie now ...'ere kettle on, I'm worn out stitching those bloody leather jockstraps all day, what a life, darlin' really...'

He was so kind to us, raw as we were from the North and uncomfortable in the rat's nest of London. He'd been in showbusiness himself when he was younger, chorus boy, session singer for 60s pop records, in the musicals, all sorts; perhaps he felt sorry for us, starting out along the old road, but, for whatever reason, he was good to us and never asked for any return. He'd take us out to piano bars, clubs and obscure discos where older men danced together, cheek to cheek. I stayed at his flat one night; it was seeping damp and chilly, a place for transients out on the unravelling edge of the city. I didn't like to think of him trailing back there in the cold, all alone and I think he often was lonely, despite being so lovable... well, you never get what you really want, ever, do you?

Eventually, of course, we came back up North. There were phone calls, cards, but then he moved, and moved again, we lost his number, the connection thinned, then severed. We were on tour, there was so much business, we meant to track him down...but we didn't.

In the end, it was the lady from the goth shop who called us. Some vicar had got in touch with her and told her Auntie was dead. He'd died of pneumonia in the sort of hostel that a priest ran in his vicarage for AIDS sufferers with nowhere to go... nowhere to go, when he could have come to us, we couldn't understand it; but apparently some friends he'd gone to when he started getting sick had turned him away in panic and he didn't want to bother anyone else in case...So in his hurt and fear he'd gone to the shelter and died amongst the cast-off furniture and the creeping smell of cabbage, Christian charity and dirty lino.

There was a memorial service at the church. We all went. It was pathetic. The vicar was very liberal, broadminded, he didn't mention hell, or sinners, he didn't have to. While he wittered on about nothing I kept thinking, Auntie would have hated this, so patronising and unctuous; we should be throwing glitter about and doing songs from the shows; I kept thinking, he's gone and I never said goodbye, I never said thank you, I never said I love you, and now I can't...except with this.

Root and Branch

She came into the café with the two children, a gust of cold air ruffling round her bare ankles and the cranky wheels of the old pushchair. I'd seen her and the little lad before in there, he's gorgeous, a real sweetheart, about seven, croppy hair sticking up in a rough gold brush, eyes of iris-blue and the breath of old Ireland in his snub nose and long upper lip. I mean cute or what...The baby, well it's a baby, a little rosy lump in a dirty top patterned with two days' spit-up rusks.

She jostled the boy into the chair opposite and parked the baby next to her. Then, having settled them, brushed back the lank swag of her long ponytail and lit a cigarette, crossing her legs and folding her arms across her breasts, face as blank as a graveyard angel. All around me, the noise softened; diners, mostly regulars in this family place, knew what was coming and like people bracing themselves against a little pain they fell silent.

She fixed the boy with a look, he stayed staring at the table. Taking another long drag, she started.

'Well, what you eating, what d'yer want you little shit, come on, come on, oh God, cat got yer tongue, eh?'

The boy didn't reply but took a toy car from the pocket of his baggy jeans and began running it back and forth. She got up stiff with rage and ordered food at the counter. In the short time it took to arrive she smoked two more cigarettes and bit her nails. The boy scuffed his huge worn-out trainers under the chair and fiddled with the little car. They ate in silence, fitfully, but after about half his food was gone he shoved the plate aside; she whipped round on him like a snake striking.

'What you doing you little shit, what's this? Bloody get that et, I paid good money for that, now you get it et.'

He whined and rubbed his face with the back of his hand.

'Not hungry, Mam...'

'Not hungry, not hungry, you'll bloody get that et when I tell yer, d'you hear me, you little shit? Look, look, see what's out there, out the window, did yer see? I saw, the Monster Man's out there, Monster Man, you don't like 'im, do yer, you're scared of 'im, ent yer? He cuts up little lads like you, like on the videos, he cuts up little lads what don't do what they're told, an' I'm going to give you to 'im, yeah I am, I'm going to give you to 'im...'

He began now to cry in earnest, scrabbling over to her and

climbing on her lap, hiding his face in her neck.

'No, Mammy, no don't Mammy, please Mammy, no...'

''Ere he is, 'ere he is, Monster Man, come and get the bad lad, haha, now yer sorry, ent yer, you little shit...'

If I'd had a gun and some way to magic those children to a safe place forever, I'd have walked over to her at that point and shot her in the head. Oh I know, I'm not stupid; she almost certainly had a rotten childhood, she's not much more than a child herself in her heart, maybe the boy is the living image of the man who did her wrong, maybe, maybe, maybe... but one thing is certain, she'll go on torturing that boy until one day he breaks and legs it with a hijacked motor, leaving her with the baby who will just about be old enough to start on, because she will do it again; it's a kick, it's a total hit, you can see it in the way she smiles, it's power, the greatest and most savage drug of all. It's the only way she ever feels any control in her life, through the certainty of his childish terror and all the glib, distancing jargon of the chattering classes can't comprehend the dumb, fucking cruelty of it.

'Now yer sorry, ent yer, you little shit, ent yer? Ooo, ooo, ooo, 'ere he comes, 'ere he comes, hah! Crybaby...'

Until last night, I didn't think he had a name but he has; his name is Liam, his name is Liam, his name is *Liam*.

You're My Friend

You're my friend and I love you; your bony face, your big nose and waterpattern eyes. I love the sideways bite of wit that you employ to keep the world at bay and you aren't easy and you don't say the things that are expected of you, folding your long skinnyness into the chair by the fire. You smoke too many cigarettes and the work you do with people whom no one else will nurse, or even admit exist, makes your pale skin waxier and more taut daily. I watch you try to be yourself in a life that would make you into something less and that's a hard battle in itself. I see you dress yourself in your nighttime clothes and hunt through clubs and bars for some dream of the truth, of a true love, that would never walk those cold halls. I see you waste your intelligence and bravery on the mundane, the uncomprehending and the stupidly malicious who drink themselves befuddled nightly in those greasy pick-up joints. They have a box for you, those people, that they would like to fold you into. The label on it says 'strong woman'; it says 'ball-breaker'; it says 'hardcase'. They think you can't be hurt so they don't try to spare you pain; I know you are easy to hurt and your hurting fills you up like a lake of poison blackening the daylight and your daily struggle to survive, making the tedious hours unbearable. I watch you gather up the threads of yourself like the drum-tight tendons in your long hands and drag yourself past the disappointment and the thoughtless nastiness with a missile comment and a one night stand, oblivion for an hour under the hands of a bastard or a fool. You're my friend and I love you; I'm not saying you're wrong, I'm not saying you're right, I'm saying the world is a bitter place for a woman like you and my heart aches for the unfairness of it.

Going Back

I went back to the house I lived in
as a child once, my grandmother's house.
The people living there were very kind,
let me look around, go into the walled garden.
They had even kept a rosebush of my nan's.
It was still blooming; great yellow and pink
peace roses, massive, velvety, just
like when I was little...

And the house seemed very small.
The mysterious and terrible darkness
at the bottom of the garden, just two
old trees bowed together shedding pine needles.
It smelt different too, of other people;
but in a faint transparency my grandmother
moved around the kitchen, my cousins,
lanky in their vanished girlhood,
chattered silently and my mother's perfume
mixed with my aunt's dark hair...

You can't go back, you can't go back;
you can only clutch at ghosts and let
the tears leak silently from squeezed shut eyes.
It never rained when you were small,
don't you remember?
Oh please, oh please, can't I
start it all again?

Not Waving

She has that pretty red hair, russet as a fox, the sort I used to think of as autumn hair, you can never quite copy it with henna; and her skin is cream-white, pinkened here and there with visible blood, the blue trace of veins clear at wrist and temple. In the face she's nice looking, always was, not beautiful, not exceptional, but her sea-blue eyes are kind and her mouth has a slight curve that looks like a cat smiling. More than one lad was disappointed when she married Phil, with his computer firm, his loud brittle jokes and his monumental tactlessness. He needs me, she said on the hen night, he needs someone to take care of him, poor thing. I thought that was a recipe for disaster and said so, but she just shook her head and said everything would be fine, everything would turn out OK. They got the semi and the patch of garden and soon the twins were born, and then the little lass, all the children favouring her auburn hair. They made the sort of happy family snap that never had Daddy in it; Daddy working away somewhere, Daddy being indispensable fixing some company system that, of course, only he understood. She had the house, she had the beat-up old hatchback, she had her little part-time job, the occasional cinema trips with us; she washed, cooked, painted the front room, took the kids to school and back and she sealed herself up inside like an oyster making a pearl. She hid everything she felt and felt guilty for feeling any-thing, she covered up the little nipping itch of rebellion against her comfy shackles with her kitty-cat smile.

White as bone her pointed face is now. I saw her last night, she looked like a mask. Her skin is layered with the burnished shadows of secret weeping and her little hands are almost transparent. I knew what it was, any woman would and almost any man wouldn't. We were all at a ridiculous party, some charity thing and it was all she could do not to throw herself into his arms. His name is Dun-can, apparently, and he is chalk and cheese with Phil being charm-ing, easy-going, handsome in that blond sporty beach bum way. He's a lifeguard at the swimming pool where we all go, that's how they met. He's not a bad boy but he's so young and when, after their summer long flirtation, he finally kissed her, this sweet, sad older woman, he broke unknowing the shimmering wall she'd built inside herself so carefully, and all the love, passion, beauty and desire that lay behind flooded her with its tragedy and its piercing joy. She can't go back, he won't go anywhere. There's gossip starting and they have evil names for her. I wanted to hug her and protect her and tell her it would all be all right even though it won't; I wanted to tell her I knew how it was and she had done her very best but she had no more control of this than of the tides or the pull of the moon. I wanted to tell her all of this but I didn't, because she was past hearing anything except the faint receding echoes of her own pain. I just kissed her dry cheek and watched her eat up her beloved with her tired eyes. I watched her know her own fate. I watched her, I watched myself and then I left, wishing she would be angry, wishing she would fight and knowing she never would, not having been given weapons for such a combat.

She was a pretty girl inside and out, as good as clean water; maiden, mother, now they'll call her whore...

I think, as I sit here drinking tea in my nice warm house, that some things, some commonplace, ordinary stupid things are unbearable, desperate and unbearable.

The Lilac

Spring budded the old lilac tree in the front garden today, the purple clusters' heavy drooping, weighing the green stems desperately; she noticed it, without thinking, by the smell, thick and sweet, as she tried to get down to the corner before her mother opened the front door, waving the airmail letter she had perfectly well seen on the hall table and tried to leave behind...it was no use.

'Soo-see, Susie dear, a letter! Look, take it with you, darling. It'll be from Nikki...Don't you want it, don't you want it? Here...good. Off you go now...what, no kiss for your old mum?'

Mother's pastel powdered face like a sugared almond turns for the cursory peck. Why does she have to wear so much make up, Susan thinks as she walks away tightly, squashing the letter into her pocket. Why did I have to get this letter today, it's not fair, I've got exams, how can I concentrate when I feel all wound up like this? Oh, I didn't want this letter, I don't want any of the letters. Why can't she just write to the parents? They'll give me the third degree tonight...she retrieves the crumpled blue paper and stares at it furiously...Where's this one from? Oh God, India; great, smashing, brilliant.

'Dear Sooz' (I hate that name, I hate it, I always did), 'here I am in beautiful downtown Goa, it's really fantastic' (of course it is, aren't all the places fantastic until she quarrels with her latest and decides it's a dump). 'James and I' (James, who's James? I thought it was Richard...) 'went to this totally amazing temple thingie yesterday, and I can't tell you what was painted on the walls, Ma would throw a complete fit, talk about porno! Anyhow...'

She crumples the flimsy sheet up, crushing the rounded childish writing with its circles for dots and stuffs it back into her pocket. I don't want to know, Nikki, I just don't want to know. I don't care about your stupid adventures and I'm sick of everyone saying how clever and daring you are, then looking at me with that sideways expression while I go red, always comparing us... all right, I'm not clever or daring, I have to make the best of this little town, drawing the edges of my life in tight and small, blocking out the light as best I can, because if I don't, who'll look after Mum and Dad when they're old? They expect someone to... Who'll take care of things? You think it's all got nothing to do with you, so you just went, running off with those scruffy friends of yours, never looking behind once. I have to grasp hold of what I can, binding myself up against the future, sister. Life is a fixed and desperate thing for me; I have it all planned, neat and inviolate. The safe job, the safe man, the unexceptional children. I can see it all, smell it, as thick and dense as the lilac, I won't leave any spaces to think in; I will shut my spirit up in an iron box and throw away the keys because how else can I survive? I know you and your chums think I'm a boring, conventional little failure; I don't dress in fashionable rags and have fashionable hair, I don't smoke dope and listen to the latest music thudding out of some skinny boy's car stereo, so you laugh at me, I know you do, I've heard you... and yes, it hurts, sister, and I'm sick of letters that make me have to lie to our parents about what you're doing as you trail around the world taking what you can and giving nothing.

I know everyone thinks I should admire you and think you're marvellous and free, but I don't. I think you're selfish and heartless, that's the truth...but no one will ever know, because I wouldn't tell anyone – they wouldn't hear me anyhow. Just leave me to turn in my small space in peace; most people lead very small lives sister, and their ambitions are small too. We are the ones who want nothing more than to get through life as best we can and die unknown...

She screws her fists round the paper hoping it will become unreadable, feeling the familiar wheeze of asthma binding at her chest. I want to be safe, I want to be safe, that's my only passion; and dragging air into her reluctant body she walks away, unknowable and savage.

Starlings

Starlings swirl round the town hall clock-tower like a ragged scarf caught by the icy wind and blown through the winter sky. It is very cold, so cold it seems that everything is made of gun metal and the burning iron of the subway railing glues itself to ungloved hands, gripping it against the deadfall icesheets.

Chris isn't wearing a coat though, despite the weather. He's got on knee-length shorts and a long-sleeve t-shirt that drags its cuffs past his red-blue knuckles, raw as horsemeat from the frost. He can cope with the cold, at least until he gets to Mick's. He does have a coat, a couple in fact, but they're beyond a joke, really, and what would he do with a coat anyway, in the club? He wants a fleece jacket but he can in no way raise that kind of cash at the moment. Money is his major preoccupation and he turns over ways and means as he slouches along, ignoring everything except the unfairness of his lot. Chris feels he could put his tousled head back and howl like a dog when he thinks about what he's got on tonight, he honestly could, but it's go out like this or stay at home and have his parents earache him about the state of the world, responsibility, et cetera, et cetera; subjects that have no meaning or interest for him whatsoever. He wishes heartily they'd get real and just give him the cash he asks for without the verbals, but Mick says that's the problem with having schoolteachers for parents, scum of the earth they are. Chris has taken to chanting that under his breath when his Mum and Dad lecture him: *scum, scum, scum, scum, scum, scum,* he goes, and they falter and give up under his blank gaze and subsonic muttering.

It's getting quite dark as Chris reaches Mick's house in a neat suburb. The door is opened by Mick's divorced mother who is just leaving, wreathed in a cloud of sneezy perfume. Chris wonders why old tarts drench themselves in that stink; he doesn't like the way she looks at him, either, as if she fancies him...retch, what a thought...wait till I tell Mick his Mum fancies me, Chris thinks, yeah, that'll get him going.

The two young men scrape up enough money to get into the club, where hundreds of people jerk through the fashionable dances ...the boys buy the correct drugs with the rest of their pocket money and get into an involved conversation with their dealer. As the dawn breaks and the starlings fly again in an inky splatter, they scratch and jitter home to curl up asleep like puppies in their unmade beds, snoring gently. They look defenceless and childlike in their oblivion, and when Chris's mother slams into his bedroom full of anger at his thoughtlessness, she dissolves weakly into tears for her lost baby, unaware that there's a thousand pounds worth of drugs hidden under his bed, stashed as a favour for a certain geezer. She sniffles all the way to work and bores her colleagues in the staffroom with how disappointed she and Gerald are with Chris, of whom great things were expected...

The day winds itself up, like every day does here, in this self-obsessed and grubby island; shops sell, the TV blurts and blares, the newspapers gossip and whine...little England, little England, Britons never, never, never, never shall be slaves... good joke, eh?

Fuel to the Flame

It takes great control to be angry. You wouldn't think so, would you; angry usually means a burst of temper, the row, the smashed plate, the nice cup of tea after the sobs and sniffs. But that's not angry, not really, that's being a bit cross, annoyed, put out. Angry is waking up every day in the certain knowledge that you can't put right the wrongs you see before you, gross and unforgivable.

Mind you, what's wrong to one person is fine to someone else, I grant you that, oh yes. I mean, when I see the Abundant Life Evangelical Church looming like a great grey warehouse on the hill, and contemplate the sorry mentality of its good Christian flock, my anger simmers a little, it must be said. Now someone else might say that Christians are decent folk with moral standards and the welfare of the world at heart and it's wrong to condemn them out of hand – even if that's what they do to everyone else; two wrongs don't make a right and all that. You can get into one of those long arguments about the state of the world that go on for hours and a clever speaker could probably beat me easily, as I was never the great debater, being too furious and prone to becoming speechless and tearful.

Because it fills me up, anger, like a balloon full of fire and it does tend to put people off, doesn't it? My gran thought I would grow out of it; 'bolshie', she said I was and when I'd had my share of knocks from life I'd settle down and mind my own business but that doesn't seem to have happened at all – in fact it's even worse as time has slowly robbed me of all my heroes. All the little cruelties and betrayals that people hand out in private with self-righteous expressions do make you understand how easily humans can do murder, rape and even genocide or the vast destructions of land and water. It's just a matter of scale. What doesn't alter is the overwhelming ability of humanity to convince itself utterly that it is justified, that it had the right, that it was someone else's fault.

You know, I remember, I remember very well when I was a child believing with all the power that I could summon, that if you loved someone enough, they would love you back, they'd have to. I was wrong, of course. But I wonder how often, in some form or other, that child's belief howls in the heart of victims when the predator looms over them, how often the tortured scream:

'You must believe me, I don't know anything, you must believe me, it's the truth', as if the truth will save them; how often the woman smashes up against the wall spitting teeth and blood crying, 'but I love you, I love you', as if her love will save her. Oh, it's not like that in real life, is it? In real life, they asked for it, they just happened to be in the wrong place, mix with the wrong people, marry the wrong man, the chain of excuses.

And it takes control to be angry, you must be precise, get hold of the twisting screaming thing each day and leash it tight, because otherwise you burn up inside and nothing gets done, you die... and what does another dead soldier mean in the great scheme of things? It means one less to be angry about the small betrayals and the great, it means one pair less of open eyes that see and cannot shut in the kingdom of the blind and that would never do, because it's a long war we're fighting against ourselves.

Nightdrive

He says, let's go for a drive, it's a good night for a drive, let's get out of here for a while. So we climb in the old car and bounce and jolt out along the cobbles, out into the city while the rain lashes the windscreen, beads it, splatters it with drops of light.

We drive through town, the late night ribbons of neon shining on the girls tottering out of the nightclubs, teetering on slippery kerbs eyed-up by thick-necked, dead-eyed bouncers; the girls giggle in short skirts and high heels, falling off their spikes, clutching onto one another, leaden in the cold coloured lights:

' 'Ere Trace, did yer...?'

'No, I never, but I could've...'

'Ooh, I could 'ave died, honest...'

The wet tarmac is a slide of treacle black, the pavements hard and hollow to the tap and click of their passage.

We turn the heater up, moving past curry houses spilling drunken boys onto the slabs, spilling them into each other and the grab and smack, the bloody nose and the plum black eye, the howl of sirens, the stop dead cop car disgorging bored policemen with better things to do:

'It was 'im what started it...'

'I never, yer lyin' toerag...'

'You pack it in, the pair of you...'

Drenched cats slither in and out of a back alley under rusty cars parked up for a party, the door of the house opening in a great exhalation of light and noise and people. The road uncoils beneath us, we could be flying, you and I, locked in this steel box and we laugh and laugh round the corners while the ghosts outside mouth and fade past us... I feed tapes into the machine, it plays *Carmina Burana* while we scream through a car wash for the crack, the green rollers like so much sea weed, the car filthy again in two minutes.

We have no good reasons.

We just want to be moving and we want to be together. We could drive forever, we could just not go back, we could go south, to the sun, the warmth, the soft air steeped in the scent of tangerines piled up against rose washed walls, we could never come back, never get pale and shrivelled again in the endless rain and the flat clip of northern voices; we could be together forever, disappear...

I say, let's just go, eh? And you grip the wheel as the car flies past boarded-up shops and concrete petrol stations garnished with racks of dead flowers that guilty men will buy for unforgiving wives. The car is big and warm, we could sleep in it easily, we could go to the sea, we could just drive, drive anywhere, through mountain passes down into deserts and we would never have to come back to this, the people, the wet gleaming city embroidered with lights and packed with people, walking, falling, living jammed together like it or not. We could be together like this forever, yes, yes... but there are too many chains, too many things we have to do, too many interlocking circles, and when we turn into our street, when we get out of the car into the rain, all the plans get sluiced away, trickle into the gutter and we don't go, we don't go this time... but one time, we will.

The Ballad of Steve and Joe

The darkness was mist-wrapped silence tracked by passing cars, water quivering on every bead-hung hedge. It wasn't cold, it would have been better if it were, this damp blanket made the long, dragging walk home even harder, as if Steve were trailing the whole earth behind him, entangling his feet in muddy snares. He knew he was drunk, not passing-out, throwing-up drunk, but enough taken to make this slow crawl seem endless. He left the car at the pub, not from any particular sense of responsibility, but because suddenly the whole thing, his whole life and its trappings seemed a burden he no longer wanted. Because I'm drunk, he thought, 'it's because I'm drunk' he said aloud to the still night, but in his heart a voice cried, 'no it's not', and he knew why.

It had been one of those evenings threaded by the promise of a party. He always went to parties, hoping secretly that they would be the great event they never were, but it was just another fat girl sobbing on his shoulder while her fiancé thrashed and grunted in a bedroom with a doll who wouldn't take off her white stilettos. He knew that, because he'd had her too, this was a small town. Girls always cried on him, though, because he was so reliable looking, and he honestly didn't mind that much. He liked women and felt sorry for this one, humiliated in public by a selfish boy. There would be a fight later, it was a sour odour brewing on the air, he could smell it, and so he was about to leave for pastures new when Joe came in...

Joe was lashed as usual, his great handsome head swinging from side to side like a bull searching for the matador, and he was in fine voice, his loud laughter killing the tinny music. His shirt was off and the light gilded his strong body only just starting to be blurred with beer fat. Suddenly, all Steve could see was Joe, Joe howling and parading through his killer clown routine, the town's pet folk devil, the drunkest, the druggiest, the irresistible Big Joe Delaney, mad and bad, his best friend, once.

Steve remembered the days when Joe had been a blade so sharp you'd cut yourself smiling as he charmed the pain away, when they'd sat in the sun planning long journeys to Morocco, Australia, America ...they were going to be heroes, pirates returning home in triumph with the golden dust of adventure glittering on them, and he'd gone, gone to that kibbutz, gone alone after listening to Joe's excuses, 'no money', 'next time, definitely, mate', 'what a piss-up we'll have when you get home!' and he'd seen the demon shudder of fear ripple Big Joe's backbone, the terror squatting behind his eyes, and he knew Joe wouldn't, couldn't make the break in case he failed, in case he wasn't King of the Castle out there, in the great world...

The girl's voice pulled him back, unwilling, she was squealing something about how awful Joe was, and was it true he...Steve gripped her by the arm so hard her breath caught and told her to shut it, while he watched his friend commit a kind of slow, public suicide with the total ruthlessness of the self-destructive, eaten up by his monstrous secret, driven by his fear, uncaring of anyone else's pain and determined to keep his worthless crown; it was horrible, and all Steve's love could not prevent it...

So he left and drove to that obscure pub, the one that everybody knew kept open, and got drunk and tried to get drunker but couldn't, no matter what he poured down his throat, while the ghost of what might have been danced just out of reach, and he left the car and walked in the sweet oblivion of the dark, letting Joe go before those drowning hands dragged him down too.

Out

The curry house is a new smart one, a bit of a cut above the usual café. One of those gas imitation log fires burns in a brass surround, and artistic photographs of traditionally dressed women hang on the white walls. We have just come out of a nightclub, the only one that would let us in, since we don't look like money. It was cheap and smelt bad, the dogged beat of the dance music banging with insane repetition, white-faced young drunks rigid with aggression searching for the excuse to attack. We stuck it for a bit, hoping it would be OK, but of course it wasn't so we left before it closed to get some food, but it was the wrong time of night. Chucking out time for everywhere else. We should have left earlier or gone straight home.

The tables around us are full of the usual sort of alcoholic, soggy, defeated, spiteful men in ugly mismatched clothes so befuddled they're unable to get a spoonful of food to their lips without spilling it down their ties. Their eyes roll in and out of focus as they squint and glare, fumbling at pockets and money. They smell of piss, booze, fags, sweat and aftershave...

The ratfaced creep opposite us heckles the teenage waiter, mumbling racist insults under his breath when the boy ignores him. It makes me so irritated I can't talk. The food is good here but I can't enjoy it; I can't enjoy anything in this town any more; I think the time has come when I don't want to deal with this constant aggravation, because I can look into their squalid, furious hearts and see myself reflected there... I do... I can feel the tingling surge of rage that wants to release itself in pain and destruction, to wipe them out because they're wrong, past salvation, repulsive and they terrify me. So I wall the feelings up again, because I know they feel the same about me and would like to see me hurt, but they haven't got the iron bands of willpower to control themselves like me, so I walk away and win this time... next time I might not be quick enough.

Memory of family

They're having a row next door, I can hear it through the wall. She's screaming at him, the senseless repetition of obscenities dropping like bricks missing their targets: he only grunts in reply. I don't know if it's her husband or her son she's raging at, I don't suppose it makes a lot of difference. I hear the door slam, it sounds as if she threw it shut after him; I imagine her hand on the dirty paint of the door, I can see her blunt hand coarsened by work, the nails blotched with lacquer, I can feel the bones beneath the reddened skin moving, articulating, the tendons stretching. I look at my own hand and flex it slowly with a kind of fear that she will move as I move, that her arm will lift when I lift mine, that our blood is flowing at the same pace, that her anger is boiling in my nerves, that my anger is pushing her to scream her useless oaths...

I walk to the mirror and see reflected a human being like all the sons and daughters of the earth that spin and trail their brief flicker of life, and in the pull of my breath I feel that infinite echo of other people breathing, as if we were all breathing together, now, all at once, like one enormous animal fractioned by accident into separate little creatures bickering, snarling and killing because of that freak severance...

I move my hand, I put it up against the mirror full span and the cold slick of the glass breaks the connection. But the memory of family remains, unreachable but visible, always visible beneath the clothes, the tribes, the savagery. The hand moves, the fingers elongate, the veins draw their blood across bone, all the same everywhere, all the same and all alone.

Romeo and Juliet

Carole was one of those people who never really get it right, you know, whatever they do, they're just naff; like, whatever she wore just looked wrong somehow and her hair was a total disaster. She always made me shiver with irritation for no definable reason, it wasn't her fault really, but she was just so, so desperate to belong, to fit in, to be liked; consequently of course, no one could stick her. Ain't that always the way?

When she took up with Vinny we were amazed, it was a nine days wonder. I mean, that boy had the worst reputation possible; he'd had every girl going and a season ticket to the pox clinic by all accounts; Carole, the perpetual virgin, was the last person on earth you'd imagine… But the months went by and they slowly became a couple, she was always running to the bar for his drinks, calling him 'Vincent', flashing the cheap silver lover's knot ring he bought her with a coy giggle and gazing at him with great big googly eyes. He just smirked a lot and accepted the hero worship as his due. It was sickening, we all used to mime sticking our fingers down our throats behind their backs and saying 'Oohh, Vincent, honestly' in her girly little voice.

Then something really dumb happened. There was a party at someone or other's, a three-dayer; Carole and Vinny got horribly stoned and swore eternal love, cementing their dopey passion by carving each other's intials into their forearms with an old penknife. Vinny made a token scratch, but Carole gave herself quite a nasty cut and ended up with some sort of blood poisoning; just the sort of idiotic thing that would happen to her, we thought. She was quite sick for a while though, and that's when the inevitable happened; Vinny strayed to pastures blonde from Leeds.

Carole went berserk. Didn't he realise she loved him? She *loved* him, he must, he just *had* to love her back as much as she adored him; it wasn't possible he didn't feel the same as her; what was he doing this for? It was a blind litany of hysteria and desperation. She threw screaming fits at him in the pub and got herself banned; she slapped the other girl when tactful Vinny showed up with her at the dance, then sobbed and threw up in the Ladies while Vinny comforted his ruffled new toy. Carole stopped eating and eventually stopped going out. Some people visited her, but just said all she did was repeat the same stuff over and over like a zombie, saying if he only knew what she was going through he'd surely come back to her... oh, he knew right enough, but it drove him off in a panic. She did all the wrong things, bombarding him daily with twenty-page letters splotched with tears, ringing him up at all hours until his mother complained to her family; it was a siege and it failed totally.

It took her six weeks. Six weeks of brooding, starving, not sleeping, and crying, crying, crying. Eventually, her parents went away for the weekend, so she sat in her room, listening to 'their song' on repeat until about three in the morning and writing the note to her family, blaming Vinny for driving her to it and begging everyone but him to forgive her. Then she took her mother's sleeping pills and swallowed the lot with Daddy's whisky. It must have hit her empty stomach like a sledgehammer; how she kept it down at first, God knows. Throwing an old coat on over her nightie, she staggered up the hill to Vinny's so he could save her, realise how he couldn't live without her and keep her safe from harm forever.

Poor silly cow, she never got it right. So hopeless. They found her in the morning stone dead, a scrawny, huddled bundle on the doorstep, sick all over her cold little face, the icy morning breeze fluttering her brown hair into feathers. She never, ever got it right ... you see, she'd been ringing his doorbell over and over, too weak to knock properly, she'd been ringing and ringing the bell while she shivered and tried to stay awake; but it didn't work, you know, the bell was broken, no one heard her; her great, grand gesture was a stupid fuck-up, her hero never even knew she was there. There was, in the end, no one to save her from herself, that inept, unloved and unlovable child we had all laughed at, so she died; not for love, no, nothing that theatrical. She died because she couldn't accept the simple, awful truth, which is: just because you love someone doesn't mean they have to love you back, it doesn't mean they owe you, it doesn't mean they're responsible for you, and you know what? Half the time it doesn't mean jack-shit to anyone but you.

Bradford Again

The kids are in the corner shop again bugging Abdul to death, their faces like white pressed cheese, gabbling round the sweet counter. They'd like to get at the alcohol better, but only being about four foot tall they can't reach that high, and anyhow, Abdul isn't stupid and while he can stand the loss of a few Crunchies, a bottle of Malibu is another matter. They quite like that stuff, the brats round here, because it tastes of Bounties and it gets you pissed quick because of the sugar content. All their mothers have got a bottle left over from Christmas; they got it given because it's dead sophisticated, like the Pink Panther lamp standard, but one swig is enough and little do they know that it's now three-quarters water since our Carl has been at it with his horrible little mates. So anyhow, Abdul has stuck all the liquor up on the highest shelf, rather like the row of porno magazines racked above the local paper; you can see 'em but you can't touch. Just as well when it comes to the mags, otherwise you'd have acne'd gangs of adolescent He-Men standing about all day fingering the merchandise and popping their spots over luscious Lucinda stuffing her overripe charms at the camera. She's into skiing and comes from Nottingham, well you would, wouldn't you?... she should be ashamed of herself, wearing that colour lingerie with that complexion, but still, you gotta earn a bob or two ain't yer?

Outside, a pit bull pisses over Carl's recumbent BMX and Marilyn and Tina are walking the babby out in the pushchair. Tina's neck is encircled with a neat chain of violet lovebites; if Tony is that passionate she'll be the next one pushing a sprog about. Marilyn is more than a bit jealous, she hardly ever sees Rick any more since the kid was born. He came round pissed up last week and give her a good smack because his mate said he'd seen Marilyn out at Blue Lace and Rick said the mother of his son shouldn't be out whoring round town and she wasn't fit to have a kid. Well, there was a bit of a go after that and Marilyn hit him with a tea mug, split his head open, so he backhanded her and she fell over the cot knocking little Lee onto the floor. He got a big lump on his head and the social worker was dead suspicious next day, nosey bitch, as if she'd do anything to hurt the precious scrap, don't he look cute in those baby jeans and that little flying jacket his nana got him off the market, like a little doll. Tina knows Marilyn is jealous, but she was stupid to fall for the kid and think Rick would wed her. Tina has already had one abortion though she had severe doubts about going through with it as her social worker said she was almost guaranteed a council flat, what with her disturbed family life and her being only just 16, but in the end she met Tone at the club and that was that, so she got rid. After all, a bloke like Tone wouldn't stick around when you were out to here with another man's kid, stands to reason. She's on the Pill now, even though Marilyn said it ain't natural, well a lot of good that attitude does her, Tina won't be caught out that way again. Tone has mentioned engagement of his own accord and you don't pass a chance like that up, he's got a job scaffolding, earns brilliant money and doesn't care how he spends it. He is a bit mental though, the other night he half killed that fella in the Tavern because he knocked over his drink. He's so strong, he got Tina by the throat once and said he'd kill her if she ever even looked at another man. He doesn't know about the abortion and he's not going to, if Tina has anything to do with it. He thought Tina was a virgin, she didn't really say she was, but she just squirmed about a bit and let on, know what I mean, and he just assumed. Well it did hurt a bit, being so soon after the op. As long as he doesn't meet up with any of her old boyfriends it'll be right. It's not likely, really, as Tone is 30 and they only go to nice clubs these days. Marilyn is jealous about that too.

The day continues, the city spreads out like an old fat woman undoing her skirt zip and dozing on the sofa, everybody's lives proceeding as they always have done since the beginning, crossing but not really touching. Still, as Tina so rightly says, it's all a go in't it? We'll all be dead in fifty years, so who gives a fuck, eh?

The Boy Nextdoor But One

The moon shines on the windows of the house
nextdoor but one, making them blind and silvery,
binding the house up tight. It's a full moon,
the lunatic asylum in town is bursting
with the wandering insane, howling while they dream
their blood has turned to gold and other nightmares.
I know this because my friend is a psychiatric nurse
and she told me. I felt like telling her,
wait another fifteen years and the boy
nextdoor but one will be in your care...

His mother was out again today,
she was screaming like some raging banshee
up the terrace, howling for the boy,
not shouting like they do round here,
'get in for your tea!' No, this was raw-throated,
roaring, foam-specked, unintelligible.
He slid from where he was hiding bonelessly,
or like a fish, waxy and resigned, offering
no resistance while she folded him into the house
again like some great, dim bird of prey.
I speak to her sometimes: she's quite unbalanced
in a normal sort of way, kind and pleasant enough
if you don't belong to her. I've been into the house,
it shrieks, it gurgles and mutters, belching out
the vegetable stink of drains blocked up,
old food, and secrets I don't want to know.
She has a husband rather in the way
some people are haunted. He appears when
he's least expected, never when he's wanted.
They don't see him often, he fathered the boy
on her, then withdrew grumbling to the pub,
the television and the attic where he keeps
his electronic keyboard, but I don't want to think
what sort of music he makes.
They never hear it anyhow, she told me,
they're not allowed up there in case the boy
breaks something. He's always breaking things.

The first week we moved in, he broke his arm
playing on our swing, I was frantic.
She came running at his scream as if
she had been waiting. Reaching him, she stooped
over the boy momentarily, like a hooded crow,
and I saw a faint, faint smile on her, like a curse.
It was the most frightening thing I've ever seen,
she might as well have eaten him up in front of us.
No latex, hydraulic, ketchup-dripping
special effect was ever a fraction
so scary as that little smile,
there and gone in an instant...
She smiled because she was happy, because
now the boy would have to stay at home
and keep her company in the house,
trapped behind the windows, growing pale and limp
behind the warped old front door.

He waves at us sometimes but hardly so as
you'd notice; his life is a pathetic promise
winding out before him like ectoplasm,
the future beckoning him like a spectre;
and I hope that one night when the moon rides
fat and glowing once again, and the wards
are overflowing with the damaged and desperate,
he won't be there too, trying for some sort of asylum.

Forgiveness

It was cold day, the air bluish with frost, breath a vapour trailing from dry lips. I think I noticed her bare legs first, mottled dull pink over lard-white flesh, her black plastic court shoes gaping from use, the heels run down. She wandered around the waiting room for a while, gazing at the governmental posters offering free contraception in the voice of the schoolroom. I don't know why she sat next to me, there were others waiting. I was reading, that usually puts people off, but she sat down, sliding to the edge of the seat tugging her short skirt down in a sad little gesture of modesty. We are all modest here, eyes downcast, we know our place, we hang on silently, ruptured virgins, soiled vessels; only the simple or the schizophrenic smile and chat to the nurses or shout and wheedle. She gave a half sob, half cough, and shaking her stiff brown perm just the colour and texture of winter bracken, she said:

'It's dead embarrassing 'ere in't it?'

I looked at her and nodded. It was all she needed, twisting the coppery wedding ring round and round her knuckly finger. The words tumbled out of her mouth like falling water:

'Oh, I could die, honest...I've never been to a place like this before, what do they do to yer? Is it awful? Oh, I feel terrible, they sent a note round to me work saying I was to come in. He'd got a dose see, the lad I'd been bothering with, he caught summat. He'd been going with other lasses as well as me, I didn't know. Still, at least he got 'em to tell me, he must think summat of me to have 'em tell me, mustn't he? Oh, when I got that letter I come over all sick, I'm married you see, not to him, like, but it's me husband, if he finds out...well, he can't at present, can he? He's inside, they can't tell him, can they, because we're married... I swear he'd kill me, he's got an awful temper. I've never been with anyone else before, honestly, but he's in for five years, I mean five years, an' it's not the first time, either. I got lonely. You do, don't you, get lonely. You want a fella's company... lasses are all right, but it's a lad you want, in't it? What d'you think?'

I said we're only human. I said I was sure it would be all right, just a check-up, nothing to fret over, though where my confidence came from I don't know, with the grim reminders of sexual disaster howling from the leaflet racks and peeling notices. But the words didn't matter to her, it was the sound of another voice she wanted, any voice that rang with that blessed medicine, forgiveness. She wanted to be forgiven, and, anonymous and distant, I was her priest, her absolution, her necessary stranger. Where she lived, out on some neglected vile estate, there was no deity for her to bribe with rosaries, the mother of Christ was not her mirror of justice, star of the sea. Hers was the unbending Protestant God of her scripture class at school who couldn't survive the world of sliced white bread, cheap cigarettes, lager, catalogue clothes and the television's eternal prattle. He was long dead and no help to her small soul.

But forgiveness must be got somewhere and if nowhere else, from an unknown woman in the pox clinic at St Luke's. I forgave her. It was easy. She smiled and I was glad to have done it, and watched her pat her hair and wipe a smudge of mascara from under her eye with her little finger. All the gestures of her confidence returned, the confessional curtain drawn behind her, her innocence and virtue strangely still intact, her placid face folded in on her salvation and her secret.

No Place Like Home

It's like water dripping on a stone, really, the water torture; drip, drip...dead slow but horribly unending, they never let up. The minute she got in today they started on her, about the company she keeps this time, surprise, surprise...twenty-two and still at home. Man, she thinks, it's no joke but it's funny, ha ha ha.

Patty lights another cigarette from the stub of the last one and notices without much surprise that her hand is shaking. The tape player auto-reverses for the second time and she can't be bothered to change the music. She knows, not just assumes – but knows that her mother is making that pinched, furious expression because the rumbling noise of the band can be heard downstairs, if not in the street. She ought to turn it down but she doesn't, so she feels guilty, but she always feels guilty about something or other so she lets it play; childish, she admits that, but so what, she's got no other vices – no lovers, she's not a druggie or a drinker, she pays her whack from what little she earns at the shop...oh, what does it matter? She begins to mimic her mother's voice talking to her father, who without doubt is taking refuge behind the evening paper.

'Listen to that, Michael, listen, the noise is dreadful, why we haven't had complaints yet I don't know. What is she doing up there all the time anyhow? It's not normal... Michael, you're not listening to me. I'm very worried, it could be drugs or anything... oh, we never had this trouble with Mark.'

Drip, drip, drip. Patty begins to laugh silently, the horrible panic feeling swelling in her like a huge balloon, she feels sick and screamy, she wants to run downstairs and shout:

'Mark? Mark? What do you know about bloody Mark? He may be your precious fucking golden boy, but he's smashed out of his brain every night and he's a complete bastard, a real bastard. Why don't you ask Sara Chatham why she had to have the abortion, Mother, and who boasted about 'getting away with it' in the pub? But he can do no wrong, can he Mother, because he went to university, played the game like he always did to your faces, and I stayed here...'

Drip, drip, drip. Jeez, Patty could see her mother's face now, and hear the grinding litany of complaints that would fall out of her parents' mouths – letting down the family, disgraceful behaviour, what will people think, swearing, and as for your clothes... oh, Mam, Mam, isn't there anything left for me? I love you. I love me Dad.

I want to love you, but you don't give me anything to hold onto. You're sealed up together like an iceberg...do you worship Mark because he left, 'treat 'em mean, keep 'em keen', is that it? I can't do it. If you're disappointed in me, Mam, then god knows I'm fucked-up because of you, and it's not my fault. It's not. Oh, the world is closing round me like a trap... animals chew their own legs off to escape the snare, don't they?

The music smashes round the little room like an anaesthetic, numbing her while she cries, heaving and retching, hugging herself into a tight ball...She'll leave soon, she knows it. But she'll never have what she craves so much, she'll go not with a proud send off, the college scarf and a blind sense of a favourite's selfish power, but furiously, and far too late, hanging on until the last minute, trying to batter down the glassy wall of her parents inability to comprehend her passion, hating them for being wrong and hating herself for her fury.

Poor child, there are other ways to hurt than with the fist or the stick, and the ones that leave no mark still leave scars just as ugly. You can love them, your Mam and Dad, but you don't have to like them, and it's when you can forgive them for their failure and their selfishness, for only being human, that can you make some life for yourself...

The Affair

I'm scared, that's what it is really,
I've thought and thought about it
until my head feels all stuffed and tight...
Can you turn the fire up? Sorry, I feel cold
all the time these days, my feet are always freezing.
No it's fear, really, is that normal?
I don't know how I'm supposed to feel.
Angry, I imagine. I do feel angry,
I was sick with fury when I first found out, you know,
I couldn't believe he'd been so weak and stupid,
that he'd let it all go on so long,
but it was all stitched up with guilt.
I felt as if I'd failed in some way,
hadn't been good enough, that it was revenge
for the bad things I'd done or something...
Oh, yes, tea would be lovely, thank you,
do you want a hand, are you sure? OK then.
No, it was no one I knew,
she's from the other end of the country.
I've seen a picture though,
skinny, pop-eyed little thing, not pretty really,
I wouldn't have thought she was his type at all,
shows how little you really know, doesn't it?
I suppose I hate her, but in a funny way,
she just seems irrelevant, horrible,
like stepping on a slug barefoot...
No, no sugar or milk, thanks, yes, dieting again,
I hate it really, but you've got to make an effort, haven't you?
All the other things, well, jealousy, stuff like that,
didn't last long; him sleeping with her,
it didn't seem to matter, honestly.
That wasn't it at all, no, oh no.
No, I'm scared, it's such a weird feeling,
I don't quite know what of;
I think, I trusted him like a child, stupid really,
and now nothing will ever be the same again,
we'll go on together and everything,
but something will have changed forever,
I won't be safe any more, somehow...

Oh thanks, I never seem to have a hanky, do I?
Sorry, I'll be all right in a minute,
probably I'm making too much fuss, I don't know.
Oh, I still love him, that's what's so hard, in a way,
you don't stop loving someone just like that, do you?
You don't stop loving someone
just because they told a lie...you can't, can you?

Kings of the World

Barry jerks awake in the reddish gloom of the living-room, his legs agonisingly stitched with cramp. For a few blank seconds he can't remember where he is; he had been entangled in a dream where his mother had been calling him for school with the insane repetition of a jackhammer. He rolls off the dusty sofa still wrapped in his doss bag and futilely tries to massage his calves. Eventually the twisting pain subsides and he staggers, unbalanced, into the kitchen, and taking a mug out of the pile of unwashed pots, he spoons some instant coffee into it and fills it up from the hot tap. He gropes for his fags and lights up, taking a savage lungful and rubbing his rough chin...*where the fuck am I?* he thinks, eyeing the greasy room ...*oh, yeah, this must be Mandy's gaff, 'course, we come here after the party...Jesus my head kills... that gear must have been dog-fucking rough...*

Upstairs, Mandy shifts about uncomfortably in the sour tangle of nylon quilts, Richie snoring into her right ear. She wishes the baby would just be born and get it over with, it's doing her head in, dragging this lump about. Thank Christ Jane gave her that huge baggy all in one, at least she doesn't have to look totally stupid... She reaches out from the mattress with a greenish white arm and fumbles about on the floor for the half-smoked joint she left there last night. Lighting it, she draws deep and shakes Richie awake. 'Go and make some tea, Rich, go on...'

'Gimme some of that first, cowbag,' he grunts, and taking the glowing stub, he stumbles downstairs in his raggy old trackie bottoms...

There's no point drawing the curtains, so they just sit in the half dark and watch TV while they do a few hot knives. Then, while Mandy goes and paints her face, the boys do a bit of whizz and share a can of lager. When Mandy appears in her purple baggy and ethnic-type skull cap, her lips as red as the broken gas fire's glow, they get a taxi into town and hit the pub where they've arranged to score some E before going on to the rave...

Days pass like this.

Weeks suck past in a fever.

Barry stays with Mandy and Rich for a couple of months, then wanders off to the Midlands because it's a happening sort of place at the moment and he doesn't want to stick around after the birth, the thought of the baby and the attendant hassle unnerves him.

Behind the fragile shelter of their imitation pride, that swaggers and brags of outlaw romance, and a fine contempt for the world and its realities, the children sit; knees pulled up and hands clamped tight over their ears, their eyes and mouths sealed shut. They rock back and forth silently... soft and weak, unable to deal with their own flawed and human selves.

Mandy's baby is stillborn. Rich goes back to his mum for the fourth time and Barry gets arrested and sent down for running someone else's coke.

Dream on. It'll be over soon enough.

Tracy

In the dusty light cast by the bus windows, Tracy could be 30, but she's actually 15; one of those people who never seem to get older but never seem to have been young. She is waxy white and thin, her hair a mousy twist that drops lankly over her scrawny neck. She has a slight cast in one eye, and the body beneath her ill-fitting tracksuit doesn't so much go in and out, as straight up and down. No one's idea of a beauty, our Trace, but she has a certain indefinable power that gives a jut to her chin and makes her the leader of her little gang. If Tracy were a dog, you wouldn't want to walk into her front yard, no, not at all. She's not clever, but like the mongrel terrier she so resembles, she's determined and she's cunning. At present she is holding forth to her entranced cronies on the subject of her forthcoming wedding, which will take place on the Saturday after her sixteenth birthday, it's all arranged.

'Look! that's the shop, that one, an' that dress in the front is the one I'm 'aving...the tight one, with the sleeves...yeah, I went in last week, din't I tell yer? I did too; mind, she's a snotty cow, her that runs it. She said to me she said, dead posh, like, 'bridesmaid's frock is it, lovey?' Well, I just give it: 'Bride, as it happens...' God, she give me a right look, an' said: 'Aren't you rather young for that?' I said, 'I'm old enough to be three months gone, and I'll look at that 'un over there, if you don't mind.' I tried it on an' it looks like like summat off the telly, fantastic. I told me mam an' she said it's mine if I want it...I mean, I'll have had the babby by then, so it should fit perfect...'

I do wonder about the hapless bridegroom at this point, while the bus jolts up the Leeds Road. What gormless Darren, Steve or Gaz strayed into Tracy's hands one hot night at the Youthie and under the sceptical gaze of her pale eyes became a daddy at 16. Too witless to make the connection, he passes from his mother to his wife without visible effort. I don't imagine it makes a lot of difference to Trace which boy she fetches up with, the male of the species is pretty superfluous to her needs, as long as he brings his wages or his dole home. In the years to come he may stray with a willing barmaid and Trace will whip down to the club sharpish and slap the girl silly to make sure the world knows what belongs to her, but it's not a jealous rage, it's simply territorial. Baz or Gaz will trail home sheepishly to face Tracy's wrath and the howling of his two little sons; or maybe he'll have a burst of independence and run off, in which case a divorce will ensue without much fuss and Tracy will hunt down another husband and marry him in the same registry office as the first one, but this time in a suit with matching bag and shoes from the catalogue.

Tracy's not daft, she's whipcord and steel. She's what patronising types like to call 'a character', which means she won't take shit off anyone, especially them. When she's a stringy old lady, her tribe will respect her infinitely more than the anonymous shadow of her consort. Certainly, no passing thug would dare to even think of mugging her for her gold creoles and her pension money. But now the bus is nearing her stop so she pulls out a smudged mirror and applies a slither of cheap lipstick to her thin mouth, fluffs up her hair and trips off the bus squeaking her trainers down the stairs and shrieking with her friends. I have a way to go and picturing the wedding makes me smile right up to home; I wish I could go, I bet it's a great do.

I Did It My Way

It's the Devil's bargain: once agreed to there's no turning back, no last minute reconciliation with God, as if He cares, no visitations from archangels with flaming swords, just you and Old Nick; him with the blood-signed parchment dangling from his sulphurous claw and you with no spit in your mouth and a grand passion to be elsewhere.

Most people don't even think about it; they are content with small lives turning in ever decreasing circles to the grave, as spotless as everyday sinners can be. Some flirt with it, thinking they can just have a little and not pay the price...they get sod all and feel cheated in some curious way, but only by themselves of course. There are always might-have-beens, could-have-beens, if-onlys: they play in local bands way past the time they should be ashamed to be seen in tight leather jeans; they wear far too much make-up and think they're Queen of some dire local haunt...They bleat about not getting the breaks, but no one listens, not that anyone listens to anyone these days, still, that's another story and I'm telling you this one tonight.

Yes, it's the Devil's bargain all right. Clear-eyed you say, OK, what the fuck, better to go out in a blaze of glory than fade away; you think you understand the coin that will buy you fame, sex, status, power, love, money, or best of all, that old elusive beauty, that smiling ikon called Art, called Creation, called the Abominable Conception, Immaculata the Whore...Oh, you say yes, yes, yes... Here's my moniker in wine dark fluid, dangerous and smoking from my veins; now give it to me quick, make me bad, make me more than anyone has ever been, make my name burn into the darkening skies for all eternity and beyond; I can take the price, whatever it might be. I am that Hero waiting for my birth into something beyond human kind; hit me with it, baby...

And it comes; not in agony; not in the savage convulsion of pain physical and understandable, no, no way, no siree.

It comes in the shop when you look into the eyes of the girl behind the counter and you see two things: fear and rejection. Small fear, little fear, just the worm's tail turning in her pupil and the thinnest veil of rejection, gossamer fine but drawn as swiftly as a blink. That's when you know...you will never join the herd again and loneliness wells up in a great howl of cold and clammy sorryness, but it's way, way too late for self pity; no use for weakness, whining or spineless grovelling now, after all, you started it ...and the plastic Madonna in her gilded shrine, she smiles that knowing smile, that Mona Lisa smirk, and you realise a spear through the heart would be easier to bear than this wolfsong in the outer dark...You got what you wanted and the Devil plays his fiddle in your soul.

Worth it? Don't make me laugh.

Regrets, I've had a stack, but then again, who hasn't?

The Velvet Glove

Jacqui – 'that's with a Q-U-I' – hugs her leather coat around her and turns the fur collar up against the autumn drizzle, stamping her little feet in their unsuitable shoes and wishing fervently she had brought a pair of gloves.

'My God,' she thinks irritably, 'why is bloody Lynn always bloody late, I definitely told her half nine; never again, honestly...'

She doesn't like standing around outside at night, it looks so common... she's already had to pointedly ignore two lots of lads with their stupid comments and cheap clothes... she makes a twisted pout of annoyance and wraps herself tighter, standing up straight, tilting her umbrella to protect her toffee-blonde ringlets.

'I'm not sure about this perm, I really am not.' She rakes and fluffs her crunchy hair, sighing as the damp begins to crimp it up then looks at her watch for the umpteenth time. It's a ladies' Rolex Danny gave her last year when he was doing well...Danny...

'Danny will be all right,' she scolds herself, 'Danny will be fine; there just comes a time when a relationship is, well, going nowhere. Now he's got no job and the Lancia's gone too, it's just pointless pretending everything's going to get better; it was only engagement, not as if we were actually married or anything; you do have to look out for yourself in this world. I mean, God knows, it's like Mum always says, no one else is going to.'

She thinks of her mother, and a curiously, blank, watchful expression smooths out her face; she has the immobility of a praying mantis, her narrow white hands clasped together while she recalls herself as a child hearing her mother's tinny screech railing against her real father, the accusations of incompetence, of sexual inadequacy, of weakness.

'You useless bastard, what have you ever done, eh, what? Tony's twice the man you'll ever be, in bed and out... he says you're queer, he's right, isn't he? You're queer, well you're no bloody man that's for sure...'

The years that followed were a roller-coaster ride of bribery or rejection; the stepfather's favour dependent on her mother's abilities to charm him physically; if all was well, Jacqui had a new car, gold chains, holidays at their villa in Corfu and cash; if things were bad, she simply didn't exist. She watched her Mum, leathery from the sun-bed and dressed twenty years too young, growing desperate and shrill. She watched her buy sex toys and humiliating lingerie at hysterical parties and found the cruel dirty videos and magazines no one bothered to conceal; she watched her mother divorce again in a savage protracted financial war, exchanging marriage for a bank balance that allowed her to buy plastic surgery to cut away the years. Jacqui watched and Jacqui learned. She armoured herself against the painful world, against softness and slipped the velvet glove over her iron hand; the staring child's great eyes closing in the deep, forgotten dark.

She comes to with a jerk as a car splatters her with gutter water.

'Oh, for Christ' sake,' she hisses, and rummages around in her bag for a cigarette, the flame of her lighter momentarily illuminating her; in the brief golden gleam she looks like a plaster saint, the bland painted surface, the ringing hollow beneath. Blinking rapidly, angrily, she pulls herself together, confused for an instant as to where she is, a ripple of panic running through her blood.

Her icy hand flutters with a tiny tremor, and looking at it, you know, tomorrow, when all she is has been reborn in daylight, it will be steady as a rock.

Ghost

It was the wind soughing through the branches that recalled for me, nothing specific, just the scent of the blood-red berries on the bushes that line the path to the hill top, the twisted pine tree's shadow that always seemed to clutch at our bare feet as we ran laughing past... Now, sitting here in the stone curve of the old wall as we did so often in the past, I try again to think it through, but all I can see is you sleeping in a white hotel room a continent away, twisting and muttering in your dreams while some strange hand tries to comfort you and fails, an unfamiliar voice threads itself into your imaginings and so wakes you, unable to trace the beat of your sealed heart.

It is very cold here now. The summers that we spent on this land are long gone and I am dizzy trying to remember just when and how we were separated. I can only see the pulse point beating in your throat and feel the hot tears drop unwilling from your dark eyes onto my mouth...there was a kiss, a terrible kiss that tore us apart and then...there is only the spin of the earth. The dusk is coming now in the heartbeat of the distant surf but it has no meaning because I can no longer move from here; as the thickening air stirs the dust and the moon gleams pale against the smoky flight of clouds, sleep flows like liquid silver, heavy, irresistible, and I conjure up your face in every detail like a talisman, before being washed into the dark.

Listen, listen, I'll meet you on the Point, high up there in the rocks and heather, and we'll be ragged dreamers scudding in the tearing wind, spit of sea foam and the cry of curlews more tangible than us, our passing won't even sway the rough grass, no one will see us as we hold hands again and we will burn away with the sunrise...

Falling

What do you know about falling?
I have it on my mind, fluttering like a bird,
its grey feathering a border
to the iron grunt of muscle,
the tension of gear that secures me to the rock.
Still I see my body, though, loose, unjointed,
swimming through the unholding air,
fingers clawed to grasp at nothing but the rising ground...
I hated being winded when I was a child
and that childishness whines up
unbidden, sickly when I think of impact;
a foolishness in the face of shattered spine
and the backless skull spilling its jellied contents
onto the greedy earth.
What do you know about falling?
I know you have missed your hold,
felt the lurching twist of a slipped foot,
known in a second's blinding gasp
that your time had come; you lived.
You show your scars,
the lumpen roots of reknotted bones
and purpled skin; you've taken
that involuntary flight and made a joke of it.
So can you take the fear from me
and laughing, throw it back aloft
like a glistening bubble, iridescent, harmless?
No, of course not and the question puzzles you.
You eat your fear and breathe it out,
grasp it in your savage hands
as it twists like a blind snake;
it is your lover, assiduously courted,
not this shadow enemy of mine...
I haul my body up on long fingers
jammed and bleeding;
I know nothing of falling and I laugh,
for once, like you.

May

The trouble with this bloody place is that everyone knows every-
one else, thinks May, as she hunches against the rattling smack of
the wind gusting off the sea. Look, there goes Mrs Elliot in that
duff Metro me Dad sold her, she'll be off to the shop now, giving
it: 'I saw your May up at the sea wall, all alone again, growing up
into a real loner, isn't she? It must be a trial to you, my dear... I
will say I wouldn't like my Janine to wear black all the time even if
it is the fashion, a bit of colour brightens a girl of her age I always
think...'

The icy air corkscrews into May's ear, hurting, and she puts up
a cold reddened hand to rub it. Ma will take on again after that I
suppose. I'd rather die than be a lardy fat cow like Elliot's Janine,
tits like jelly balloons wobbling out of something tight and pink
from the catalogue and great fat thighs like tinned ham, I'll never
forget those cycle shorts last summer, she's not right in the head...
and that voice, dead refined:

'Oo-er, 'ere, May, gorra fella yet? Yer so wee-erd you, ent yer?
Eh? 'Ere, you a gothic, May, like wot was in the Sun last week?
'Ere, girls, May's a gothic, well there 'ent no gothic lads round
'ere, so poor old May, eh?'

I shall smack Janine up the side of her stupid painted face one
day, May vows. I'd rather be 'wee-erd' than the village bike. Mind
you, she'd have to be in labour before she realised she was up the
stick with that gut on her. I wonder if the vicar ever wonders what
all that squealing in the graveyard at night is... too busy wanking
about the Cubs probably, the dirty old sod, as if we didn't all know
... May squints as the waves splatter her with a whip of spray.
Going to be a blow on tonight, she thinks. The sea is indigo and
the great grape-dark clouds belly downwards, heavy with sleet.

Shepherd's pie tonight, it's always shepherd's pie on Mondays,
it always will be shepherd's pie on Mondays. I can't eat it. I don't
want to eat it, all glutinous and gristly with Smash on top... I don't
want to eat ground up bits of dead animal, but try telling that to
the family. I can see Gareth now, the pig:

'Give it 'ere then, sis, I'll 'ave it...' Shoving it down his throat
without it touching the sides. Dad spitting carrots all over and
pointing at me with his fork: 'Don't be so ungrateful for good food,
girl, you could do with a bit of meat on them bones, and a few
less airs and graces if you don't mind...'

He thinks I'm being snotty for the sake of it, they all do, but it's not that. I just want something that isn't all the village and everyone being related and everyone trying to force you into the same mould as themselves, trying to skin you alive then push you into a *good girl*'s skin, just so long as you look the same as them and say the same things, forever and ever, until you're dead, and you may as well never have been alive. It's like they're just waiting to die, just passing the time, as if feeling things, thinking things, was horrible and dangerous, as if wanting to be really alive was dirty and disgusting... Oh, I don't know, it just seems such a stupid waste, existing like they do... Oh God, I could get run over tomorrow and I won't have been anywhere or done anything...

She can see the blue veins lumpy on her freezing hand: I don't think I've got the same blood as them, she thinks, jumping down onto the shingle and crunching back towards the village. I think a gypsy had it off with me Ma and she's not letting on... The picture of her mother in a passionate embrace with a dark stranger, with anyone, really, starts the giggles running through her blood. Not me Ma, she thinks hysterically, not me Ma, not even with me Dad. 'Pull me nightie down when you've finished, Brian...' I must have been an immaculate conception, must have been, that means I'm God:

'I'm God, me!' she screams into the wind, just as Tony Elliot walks round the corner. May chokes a gargled ''Lo, Tone', but he just gives her a funny look and walks on. Oh, what the fuck, May thinks, I'll go and see Sand, she's all right even if that lad of hers does hate me... there must be more to life than this, there must be, there will be, I'll rip the whole world up and shape it into what I want, I'll make something happen...

And she walks, hands stuffed into her leather jacket pockets, into the growing gale.

Last Words...

'If I should die, think only this of me...'

I didn't snuff it from an infected midge bite in some corner of a foreign field, but from having my lights punctured by a starving knifeman in Rio who spilt my claret for the sake of a pearlised silver plastic mugger trap wallet and a pair of gold sleepers from Ratners. Dead, dead and only the cat ever called me *Mother*.

As my lily-draped catafalque sways down Leeds Road bearing its tragic burden, the air rent by the howling cries of the grieving throng, dwell momentarily on my sterling qualities: those shining attributes that stood me head and shoulders (literally) above the heaving, sweating mêlée of the common herd, that pustulant excrescence that we laughingly dub 'humanity'...think of my all-encompassing guilt, my savage megalomania, the ready tears, the readier sarcasm, that whip-like tongue ever happy to lash the unfortunate and insufferable fool and last, but by no means least, the temper...ah! Remember its super nova flare, a bright flash searing all in its path then burning out in a millisecond leaving only a crumpled me sobbing over the ashy remains.

Yes, think of me, oh horseman riding by; rein up your malevolent, wall-eyed lump of equine devilmeat and cogitate upon this scarlet haired witch queen, this tattooed termagant, this five-year-old teddy bear with an attitude problem...

Remember me, the monster of my own creation, the phantom at the feast; the grey-eyed looker-on, soft, warm, cuddly with muscle and woman fat, fragrant with fresh sweat and expensive soap, snotty, tired and spotty, the farting, coughing hag grasping at the fleeing years with iron claws, no better and no worse than the worst and best.

I had beautiful hands and feet. I breathed the air that you breathe now, you are breathing my last exhaled breath; I will never die because I will never be forgotten entirely.

I loved you with all the fierce and savage love of the unwanted child. I loved you as I stared in your lighted windows from the cold streets. I loved you and wrote about you with some skill and a deal of passion. I drew your faces, wizened, beautiful, taut-skinned or fleshy. I died as you will, a testament to mortality... and for the sake of my ghost, don't bury me in Bradford...